BBC

DOCTOR WHO

THE THIRTEENTH DOCTOR

"As the Doctor would say, brilliant!"
BIG COMIC PAGE

"I can't say enough good things about this. It's everything that *Doctor Who* does best."
BUT WHY THO?

"This is one book newcomers and old fans alike are sure to enjoy. 9/10!"
EXPLORE THE MULTIVERSE

"This comic captures the energy and dramatic elements of the recent *Doctor Who* series. All of the creative team work together to produce a solid adventure which is sure to win the hearts of the fans."
MONKEYS FIGHTING ROBOTS

"Perfectly captures the look and voices of the characters!"
ADVENTURES IN POOR TASTE

"If you're a fan overflowing with love for the new Doctor, this is a great place to get an extra dose of *Doctor Who*."
COMICBOOK.COM

"Highly recommended... Bold, sassy, intelligent, and accessible to new fans. 5 out of 5!"
GEEK SYNDICATE

"A perfect continuation of what we've come to love about Series 11. 5 out of 5!"
KABOOOOOM

"A radical romp through time and space!"
NERDIST

"Houser nails it."
NEWSARAMA

"The art team continues to excel!"
SCIFI PULSE

Doctor Who Backlist

See Reading Order for full list of titles

TENTH DOCTOR: YEAR ONE
Hardback: 9781785863998

ELEVENTH DOCTOR: YEAR ONE
Hardback: 9781785864001

TWELFTH DOCTOR: YEAR ONE
Hardback: 9781785864018

Editor
Jake Devine

Senior Designer
Andrew Leung

Titan Comics

Managing Editor
Martin Eden
Senior Creative Editor
David Leach
Production Controller
Peter James
Senior Production Controller
Jackie Flook
Art Director
Oz Browne

Sales & Circulation Manager
Steve Tothill
Publicist
Imogen Harris
Press & Publicity Assistant
George Wickenden
Ads & Marketing Assistant
Bella Hoy
Commercial Manager
Michelle Fairlamb

Head Of Rights
Jenny Boyce
Publishing Director
Darryl Tothill
Operations Director
Leigh Baulch
Executive Director
Vivian Cheung
Publisher
Nick Landau

For rights information contact Jenny Boyce
jenny.boyce@titanemail.com

Special thanks to Chris Chibnall, Matt Strevens, Sam Hoyle, Mandy Thwaites, Suzy L. Raia, Gabby De Matteis, Ross McGlinchey, David Wilson-Nunn, Kirsty Mullan and Kate Bush for their invaluable assistance.

BBC Studios

Chair, Editorial Review Boards
Nicholas Brett
Managing Director, Consumer Products and Licensing
Stephen Davies
Head of Publishing
Mandy Thwaites
Compliance Manager
Cameron McEwan
UK Publishing Co-Ordinator
Eva Abramik

DOCTOR WHO: THE THIRTEENTH DOCTOR: TIME OUT OF MIND
ISBN: 9781785868894

Published by Titan Comics, a division of Titan Publishing Group, Ltd. 144 Southwark Street, London, SE1 0UP.

A CIP catalogue record for this title is available from the British Library.
First edition: February 2020.

10 9 8 7 6 5 4 3 2 1

Printed in Spain

BBC

DOCTOR WHO

THE THIRTEENTH DOCTOR

WRITER
JODY HOUSER

ARTISTS
ROBERTA INGRANATA
GIORGIA SPOSITO
VALERIA FAVOCCIA

COLORISTS
ENRICA EREN ANGIOLINI
TRACEY BAILEY

COLOR ASSISTANT
SHARI CHANKHAMMA

LETTERERS
RICHARD STARKINGS &
COMICRAFT'S JOHN ROSHELL, SARAH
JACOBS & SARAH HEDRICK

TITAN COMICS

BBC

BBC

DOCTOR WHO

THE THIRTEENTH DOCTOR

PREVIOUSLY...

The Doctor and the gang have been on many wild, fantastical, and often dangerous trips across the myriad planets and galaxies throughout time and space. They've thwarted the nefarious plots of devious aliens, experienced different cultures and civilizations in history, and made many friends and allies along the way. Now it's time for a little break, the only way the Doctor knows how...

The **Doctor**

The Thirteenth Doctor is a live wire, full of energy and fizzing with excitement and wit! The Doctor is a charismatic and confident explorer, dedicated to seeing all the wonders of the universe, championing fairness and kindness wherever she can. Brave and selfless, this Doctor loves to be surrounded by friends!

Ryan Sinclair

Ryan is 19 years old, born and bred in Sheffield. He works in a warehouse while studying to become a mechanic. He likes video games and is great with technology! Ryan is dyspraxic, which means he sometimes finds physical co-ordination tricky – but his curiosity and energy always win out over fear.

Yasmin 'Yaz' Khan

Yaz is a 19-year-old Sheffielder, friendly and self-assured, a quick logical thinker and a natural leader – the perfect person to have around in a crisis! Yaz loves her job as a probationary police officer, but wants more – not because she's bored, but because she loves adventure and the thrill of the new!

Graham O'Brien

Graham is a funny, charming and cheeky chap from Essex – he's a family man and an ex-bus driver, with a sharp sense of humor and a caring, warm nature. He might be of a different generation (and might sometimes move at a slower pace than Yaz and Ryan), but he's brave, selfless, and wise too – just like the Doctor.

The **TARDIS**

'Time and Relative Dimension in Space'. Bigger on the inside, this unassuming blue police box is your ticket to amazing adventures across time and space! The Doctor likes to think she's in control of her temporal jaunts, but more often than not, the temperamental TARDIS takes her and her friends to where and when they need to be...

ALRIGHT GANG. TODAY IS THE TARDIS'S PICK.
EVEN MORE SO THAN USUAL, I MEAN.
LET'S SEE WHAT'S BEYOND THOSE DOORS, SHALL WE?
MYSTERIES TO SOLVE? WORLDS TO SAVE? SNACKS? GETTING A BIT PECKISH...
POLICE BOX

SNACKS ARE LOOKING TO BE A SAFE BET, DOC.

ALTHOUGH IF IT'S ANYTHING LIKE EARTH, THEY'LL BE *VERY* OVERPRICED.

COULD BE SOME KIND OF EVIL AMUSEMENT PARK, YEAH?
LIKE THE CARNIVAL IN THAT BOOK?
SOMETHING WICKED THIS WAY COMES. RAY BRADBURY. LOVELY MAN.
BIT DISAPPOINTED WHEN I SHOWED HIM WHAT MARS WAS *REALLY* LIKE.
WHY HAS THE *TARDIS* BROUGHT US HERE? DOES SHE THINK WE'RE DUE A HOLIDAY?
DOES THE TARDIS EVEN *DO* HOLIDAYS?
ON OCCASION. RARELY GOES WELL. USUALLY A PROBLEM WITH DOUBLE-BOOKED ROOMS.

ONLY ONE WAY TO FIND OUT WHY...

THIS LOOKS PROMISING...

ADMISSION FOR FOUR PLEASE.

ULTIMATE SUPREME CLASS MULTIGUEST PACKAGE!
OF COURSE, OF COURSE!

RIGHT THIS WAY, MOST HONORED MULTIGUESTS!
COULD YOU GET US INTO DISNEY WITH THAT THING?
OF COURSE I COULD, *RYAN*.
THAT IS WHERE I MET *BRADBURY*.

AND SO THE FUN BEGINS...

THIS LOOKS ABOUT MORE MY SPEED...

DO I NEED SOME SORT OF TICKET TO PLAY?
ALL MULTIGUESTS WELCOME.
win prizes

VERY BEST OF LUCK TO YOU.

USED TO BE PRETTY GOOD AT THROWING THE OLD BALL.
AREN'T THESE SORTS OF GAMES ALWAYS RIGGED ON EARTH?

USUALLY. BUT DOESN'T MEAN THAT'S THE CASE *HERE*.

DO I GET ANOTHER--

ISN'T THAT SOMETHING?

IS SOMETHING WRONG, DOCTOR?
NOT SURE, YAZ. THERE'S SOMETHING...
IT'S *RIGHT* ON THE TIP OF MY BRAIN.

HUH. SUPPOSE THAT WAS IT.

GOOD SHOW, GRAHAM.
I THINK THAT'S ENOUGH GAMES FOR THE MOMENT.
EVERYTHING OKAY, DOCTOR?

YOU CANNOT LEAVE! THAT MULTIGUEST LOST!
THEY WILL BE TRANSFERRED TO THE PRIZE POOL!

PRIZE POOL? WHAT DOES THAT--
UM, DOC...
NO!
GRANDDAD!

DID HE JUST--
SHORT-RANGE TELEPORT. HE SHOULD BE OKAY.

"WHEREVER HE WAS JUST SENT."
IS SOMEBODY THERE?
CAN YOU TELL ME WHERE I AM?

OH, HELLO THERE. DID YOU GET STUCK HERE TOO?
NO NEED TO WORRY. I HAVE A FRIEND WHOSE SPECIALTY IS GETTING PEOPLE OUT OF SCRAPES.

"I'M SURE SHE'LL BE ALONG ANY MINUTE..."
BEVIVIAN GAMES OF CHANCE. I REMEMBER NOW. VERY HIGH STAKES.
WHAT ARE YOU DOING IN A FAMILY ESTABLISHMENT LIKE THIS?

I VIOLATED NO LAWS HERE! THEY CHOSE TO PLAY!

AND BY THE LAWS OF MY PEOPLE, YOU'RE A KIDNAPPER.
WE'VE DEALT WITH KIDNAPPERS BEFORE. IT REALLY DIDN'T END WELL FOR THEM.

NO KIDNAPPING! MULTIGUESTS AGREE TO RULES ON ENTRANCE!
AND THE BEVIVIAN RULES SAY IF WE WIN YOUR GAME, WE GET OUR FRIEND BACK.
AND WHOEVER ELSE MAY HAVE BEEN ROPED IN BY YOUR SHINY BALL.
YOU'RE WELCOME TO TRY.
I'M BETTING YOU WERE RIGHT WITH WHAT YOU SAID BEFORE, RYAN.
THE GAME IS MOST DEFINITELY RIGGED.
THEN HOW DO WE GET HIM BACK, DOCTOR?

I'VE BROUGHT YOU LOT ACROSS TIME AND SPACE. WE'VE DONE *BRILLIANT* THINGS TOGETHER.
YOU'RE MY FRIENDS. AND I'M RESPONSIBLE FOR YOU.

I'M NOT ABOUT TO LET A *SINGLE* ONE OF YOU GET EATEN BY A THIRD-RATE CARNIVAL GAME.

I'M GOING TO RESCUE YOUR GRANDDAD. AND YOU'RE GOING TO HELP ME.
YOU'LL KNOW WHEN.

ALRIGHT, THEN. GUESS I'LL GIVE IT A GO.
ONE THROWBOT, IF YOU PLEASE.

DID I EVER TELL YOU ABOUT THE TIME I MET BABE RUTH?
GAVE ME SOME GREAT ADVICE.
VWRRRRRRRR
NO! THAT ISN'T--
POSSIBLE?
BY YOUR OWN RULES, I WON THE GAME.
NOW. GIVE MY GRANDDAD BACK.
VWRRRRRRRR

FINE.
AH! SEE THERE?
TOLD YOU MY FRIEND WOULD SORT IT ALL.
BRILLIANT JOB, RYAN.
GO HUG YOUR GRANDAD.

DON'T WORRY. WE'LL HELP YOU FIND YOUR PARENTS.
I MEAN, IF YOUR PLANET HAS PARENTS.
THREE OF THEM. AND THEY'LL BE VERY WORRIED.
AS FOR YOU, I'D PACK THINGS UP. FIND A NEW LINE OF WORK.
ONE THAT DOESN'T INVOLVE COLLECTING PEOPLE.
I'LL BE KEEPING AN EYE ON YOU FROM NOW ON.
WHO ARE YOU?

I'M THE DOCTOR. THESE ARE MY FRIENDS.
AND THIS IS WHAT WE DO.

A FEW TIME-JUMPS LATER...
"RIGHT. SO. HOLIDAYS!"
SHOULD DO SOMETHING SPECIAL TO CELEBRATE, RIGHT?
WHERE WOULD YOU LIKE TO GO?
RYAN AND ME, WE DO HAVE A CHRISTMAS DINNER TO GET TO...
TIME MACHINE, GRAHAM.
WE CAN FIT IN ALL THE PLANS WE WANT, AND THEN SOME.
RIGHT, RIGHT. JUST AS LONG AS I DON'T SHOW UP TO DINNER LOOKING A DECADE TOO OLD, I SUPPOSE.
LOT OF QUESTIONS, THERE.

WHAT ABOUT DISNEYLAND?
OR COOL, *FUTURE, OTHER PLANET* DISNEYLAND.

I CAN'T BELIEVE YOU'D WANT TO GO BACK TO A THEME PARK AFTER WHAT HAPPENED LAST TIME.
YEAH BUT, WE JUST WON'T GO TO *THAT* ONE.

WELL, WE'LL JUST MAKE SURE GRAHAM DOESN'T GET EATEN UP BY A RIGGED GAME THIS TIME.

DOC...
...WHAT ARE YOU TALKING ABOUT?

WHAT?

I KNOW WE'VE DONE A LOT OF STRANGE THINGS WITH YOU, DOC...
...BUT I THINK I'D REMEMBER GETTING EATEN.
THE AMUSEMENT PARK.
THE BEVIVIAN GAME OF CHANCE.
"YOU SPLIT OFF FROM US TO PLAY FOR A BIT.
PUBLIC CALL
"GOT TELEPORTED AWAY BY THE THROWBOT WHEN YOU LOST.
"LUCKY THING I WAS ABLE TO RIG THE GAME RIGHT BACK. GET YOU AND THE OTHER 'PRIZES' OUT OF STORAGE."

THAT'S... NOT AT ALL WHAT I REMEMBER, DOC.

I'M SURE IT'S A BIT DIFFERENT ON THE OTHER END OF THE TELEPORT...
BUT I DON'T REMEMBER ANY OF THAT. NOT THE GAME, NOT THE TELEPORT.

RYAN WAS THE ONE WE HAD TO RESCUE.
WHAT? ME?

"YOU WENT INTO SOME SORT OF ALIEN HAUNTED HOUSE.
"EXCEPT IT WAS FULL OF ACTUAL GHOSTS. AND WE HAD TO KEEP YOU FROM BECOMING ONE."

WELL THAT SOUNDS RIGHT CREEPY.
GLAD IT DIDN'T ACTUALLY HAPPEN.

BUT I REMEMBER IT ALL SO CLEARLY...
THANK YOU, RYAN.

SORRY, DOCTOR...
...BUT I DON'T REMEMBER WHAT *YOU* TOLD US ABOUT HAPPENING EITHER.

WELL, THIS IS ODD.
AND NOT NECESSARILY THE *FUN* SORT OF ODD.
YAZ, DO YOU REMEMBER THINGS DIFFERENTLY AS WELL?
I DO, YES.
BUT YOU *DO* REMEMBER THE AMUSEMENT PARK.
TELL ME WHAT YOU *BOTH* THINK HAPPENED THERE.

"THERE WAS THIS ALIEN CLOWN, YEAH? HAD ONE OF THOSE TRICK FLOWERS.
"ONLY IT WASN'T WATER IT SPRAYED.
"WE BARELY FOUND THE ANTIDOTE FOR YAZ IN TIME."
TOTALLY DIFFERENT FROM WHAT I REMEMBER.
"THE DOCTOR PLAYED ONE OF THOSE GAMES THAT TESTS YOUR STRENGTH.
"AND SHE DID IT SO WELL THAT THEY PUT HER IN THEIR GLADIATOR GAMES."
ALL RIGHT, NOW WE'RE JUST GETTING SILLY.
IT'S BEEN DECADES SINCE I WAS A GLADIATOR.

SO WE HAVE FOUR DIFFERENT VERSIONS OF EVENTS. A DIFFERENT SET OF MEMORIES FOR EACH OF US.
BUT THERE'S ONE THING MISSING FROM MY MEMORIES.
WHAT'S THAT, DOCTOR?
THE NAME OF THE PLANET WE WERE VISITING.
CAN ANYONE ELSE REMEMBER IT?
NO, I DON'T.
ME NEITHER.
WE DO VISIT A LOT OF PLANETS, TO BE FAIR.
WELL, THERE'S SOMEONE HERE WHOSE MEMORIES CAN'T BE ALTERED.

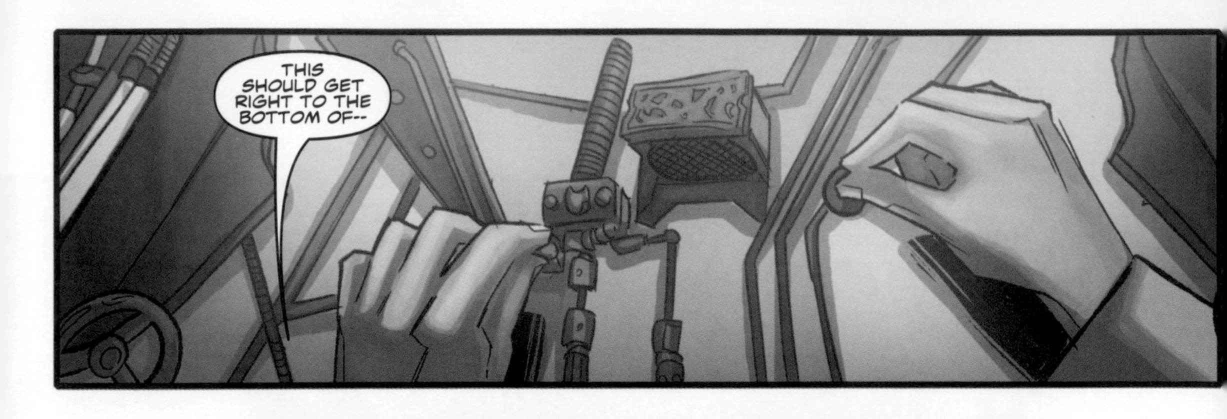
THIS SHOULD GET RIGHT TO THE BOTTOM OF--

...THAT'S IMPOSSIBLE.
WHAT IS IT?

NOTHING. ABSOLUTELY NOTHING.

THE TARDIS HAS NO RECORD OF WHERE WE WERE THAT DAY.

HOW CAN SOMEONE ERASE INFORMATION FROM THE *TARDIS?!*
...AND FROM US TOO, I GUESS.

I'M NOT ENTIRELY SURE.
AND I'M HONESTLY A BIT MORE CONCERNED ABOUT THE WHY THAN THE HOW.
"SOMEONE WENT THROUGH A LOT OF TROUBLE TO GIVE US NOT JUST NEW MEMORIES...
"...BUT RATHER UPSETTING MEMORIES."
TO SCARE US AWAY?
PERHAPS IN PART. BUT IT'S ALSO LIKELY THAT THE MEMORIES THAT WERE REPLACED WERE OF... SIMILAR TONE.
EASIER TO OVERLAY ONE UPSETTING MEMORY WITH ANOTHER THAN TO TRY AND EXPLAIN AWAY THOSE FEELINGS.

WE JUST HAVE TO RETRACE OUR STEPS.
BEST THING TO DO WHEN YOU LOSE SOMETHING, RIGHT?
I'M NOT SURE WE *LOST* THE MEMORIES AS MUCH AS HAD THEM *TAKEN*...
NO, I THINK GRAHAM HAS THE RIGHT OF IT.
I MAY NOT HAVE A NAME OR COORDINATES. ANY RECORDS.
BUT I AM QUITE GOOD AT REMEMBERING STARS. JUST NEED TO DO A BIT OF TRIANGULATION.
"IF SOMEONE WANTS US TO STAY AWAY...

"...I'D LIKE TO KNOW WHY."

RATHER GRIM SORT OF PLACE, ISN'T IT?

I LIKED THE NIGHTMARE AMUSEMENT PARK A BIT MORE, I THINK...

COULD YOUR MEMORY OF THE STARS HAVE BEEN ALTERED TOO?

PERHAPS. BUT EITHER WAY, *SOMETHING* LED US HERE.

VWOOORPP VWOOORPP

AND I'M GOING TO FIND OUT WHAT.

VWORP
VWORP

DEFINITELY NOT AN AMUSEMENT PARK.
POLICE TELEPHONE
FREE FOR USE OF PUBLIC
ADVICE & ASSISTANCE OBTAINABLE IMMEDIATELY
OFFICERS & CARS RESPOND TO URGENT CALLS
NICE, THOUGH.

RATHER FESTIVE SORT OF PLACE.
WHERE IS EVERYBODY?
SUPPOSE WE'LL SEE IF ANYONE'S HOME...

HELLO?
RAP RAP RAP
GO AWAY!
SOMEONE'S HOME.

RAP
MY NAME IS THE DOCTOR. I'M HERE WITH SOME FRIENDS. ALL VERY LOVELY PEOPLE.
WE DON'T WANT TO CAUSE ANY TROUBLE. WE JUST HAVE A FEW QUESTIONS.
RAP RAP

DON'T YOU THINK YOU CAUSED US ENOUGH TROUBLE?

THAT'S SORT OF THE RUB OF IT.
I SUSPECT WE'VE BEEN HERE BEFORE. BUT NEITHER MY FRIENDS NOR I HAVE MEMORIES OF IT.
WELL, WE *HAVE* MEMORIES. BUT THEY'RE ALL THE WRONG SHAPE. AND NONE OF THEM MATCH.
SOMEONE TRIED TO MAKE SURE WE'D NEVER WANT TO COME BACK TO YOUR WORLD AGAIN.
WHICH SOUNDS RATHER LIKE WE EITHER CAUSED QUITE A BIT OF TROUBLE... OR TRIED TO STOP IT.

AND I KNOW WE'RE GENERALLY MORE IN THE TROUBLE-STOPPING BUSINESS.

COME INSIDE! HURRY.
BOK

SHOULDN'T HAVE COME BACK. SHOULDN'T HAVE COME BACK.
CAN YOU TELL US WHAT HAPPENED LAST TIME?
AND WHO MESSED WITH OUR MEMORIES AND OUR SHIP'S RECORDS?
THAT WOULD BE...
...IT WAS PROBABLY...
MR. HENDERSON.
MR. HENDERSON?!
NOT AN ALIEN SORT OF NAME, IS IT?
HAD A MS. HENDERSON AS A MATHS TEACHER YEARS AGO.
...BUT SHE WAS ALWAYS NICE. AND ON EARTH. PROBABLY NOT THE SAME ONE.
WHAT CAN YOU TELL US ABOUT THIS MR. HENDERSON? AND WHERE CAN WE FIND THEM?

OH, MR. HENDERSON SCRAMBLED YOUR HEAD RIGHT GOOD, DIDN'T HE?
WHAT MAKES YOU SAY THAT?
BECAUSE YOU ASKED ME THE SAME QUESTION LAST TIME YOU WERE HERE.
AH. I SEE.
WHY DON'T WE START AT THE BEGINNING?
WHAT HAPPENED THE LAST TIME ME AND MY FRIENDS WERE HERE?
WELL...
YOU MUST PROMISE NOT TO TELL MR. HENDERSON.
WE PROMISE.

"YOUR LITTLE SHIP ARRIVED IN OUR VILLAGE THAT DAY.
POLICE PUBLIC CALL BOX
"WE THOUGHT THAT IT HAD BEEN SENT BY MR. HENDERSON.
"SO THOSE WHO WERE TO BE OFFERED GATHERED, AS THEY ARE SUPPOSED TO."
WHAT DO YOU MEAN, "THOSE WHO WERE TO BE OFFERED"?
THOSE WHO WILL GO TO WORK ON MR. HENDERSON'S WORLD.
THOSE WHO GO -- AND NEVER COME BACK.
THOSE ARE THE EXPRESSIONS YOU MADE WHEN I TOLD YOU THIS THE LAST TIME.

LET ME GUESS.
I ASKED YOU FOR ALL THE INFORMATION YOU HAD ON THIS MR. HENDERSON AND SAID I'D GET YOUR PEOPLE BACK.

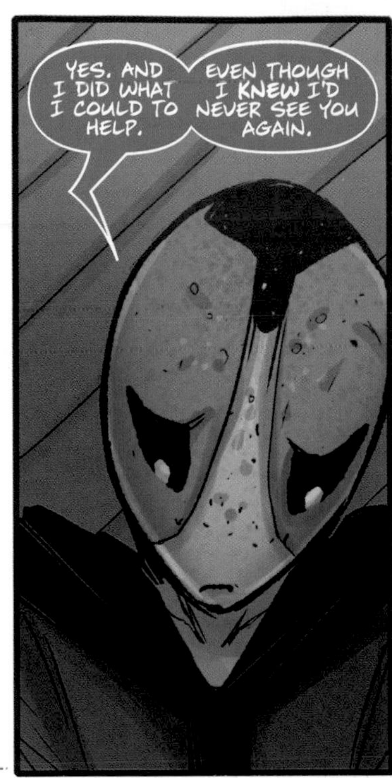
YES, AND I DID WHAT I COULD TO HELP.
EVEN THOUGH I KNEW I'D NEVER SEE YOU AGAIN.

ONE LITTLE PROBLEM WITH THAT, UM...

I'M SORRY. I DON'T ACTUALLY REMEMBER YOUR NAME.

FRIFFLE.

YOU CAN SEE US AT THIS VERY MOMENT, FRIFFLE.
AND THAT MEANS AGAIN IS RIGHT NOW.

ONE QUESTION, DOCTOR...
IF THE LAST TIME WE DID THIS, WE GOT OUR MEMORIES MESSED WITH, HOW DO WE KNOW IT WON'T HAPPEN AGAIN?
BECAUSE THIS TIME, RYAN, WE'LL BE READY FOR IT.
THIS *IS* ONLY OUR SECOND VISIT TO YOUR WORLD, RIGHT?
THAT IS CORRECT.
COMPLETELY AND TOTALLY PREPARED.
NOW, FRIFFLE. PLEASE TELL US EVERYTHING YOU TOLD US LAST TIME.
AND EVERYTHING YOU ***WISH*** YOU HAD TOLD US LAST TIME...

"ALL RIGHT. PRECAUTIONS."
I MADE THESE NEUROLOGICAL TRACKERS TO MONITOR OUR BRAIN ACTIVITY.
IF ANYTHING SUSPICIOUS HAPPENS, THEY'LL LIGHT UP.
INFORMATIVE AND FESTIVE.
IS THAT... ARE YOU OKAY WEARING THAT?
I'M MUSLIM. WE'RE NOT EXACTLY ALLERGIC TO TINY LIGHTBULBS.
HA! RIGHT.

DO YOU THINK THIS COULD BE THAT HOARDER FELLOW WE KEEP RUNNING INTO?
HE WAS PRETTY KEEN ON FORCING PEOPLE TO WORK FOR HIM.
THE HOARDER WAS MORE ABOUT TIME TRAVEL FOR PERSONAL PROFIT.
I DIDN'T SEE ANY SIGN THAT FRIFFLE'S PEOPLE HAD ACCESS TO THAT SORT OF TECHNOLOGY.
AND UNFORTUNATELY, THERE ARE FAR TOO MANY BEINGS IN THIS UNIVERSE WHO TAKE ADVANTAGE OF OTHERS LIKE THAT.
KEEPS ME BUSIER THAN I WISH...
KEEPS *US* BUSY, YOU MEAN.
MIGHT AS WELL DO SOME GOOD WHILE TOURING TIME AND SPACE, YEAH?

MY FAM.
CAN'T SAY I DIDN'T CHOOSE WELL.
HOLD ON, EVERYONE!
TO THE RAILINGS AND YOUR BRAINS.
ARE WE WORRIED ABOUT LOSING MORE THAN JUST MEMORIES HERE?
JUST FOR REFERENCE...

VWORP
VWORP
POLICE PUBLIC CALL BOX

WELL. CAN'T SAY THAT THIS IS WHAT I EXPECTED.
POLICE PUBLIC CALL BOX
POLICE TELEPHONE
PULL TO OPEN

HUH.
WAIT, IS THAT--

DID WE CIRCLE BACK AROUND TO EARTH SOMEHOW?

DESPITE WHAT IT MAY LOOK LIKE, YAZ...

POLICE PUBLIC CALL BOX
POLICE PUBLIC CALL BOX
...THIS IS DEFINITELY NOT EARTH.
WELL, LET'S HAVE A LOOK.

FEELS CRAZY TO EVEN ASK THIS, DOCTOR...
...BUT IS SANTA, YOU KNOW... *REAL?*
WHAT DOES REAL EVEN MEAN?
CHILDREN ALL OVER THE WORLD BELIEVE IN SANTA. WRITE HIM LETTERS. SEND HIM THEIR WISHES.
BY SOME MEASURES, YOU COULD SAY THAT SANTA IS *MORE* REAL THAN ANY OF US.
NOTICE SHE TOTALLY DIDN'T ANSWER THE QUESTION.
RAP
WAAAH WAAH WAAAH
OOPS?

SLAM
OOF!
SPIES!
REALLY MORE TOURISTS THAN SPIES...

WHAT'S GOING ON?

WHAT ARE THEY DOING HERE?
...SANTA?!

WHAT DID YOU SAY?!
UM. NOTHING?

IS THAT SOME SORT OF BAD WORD IN THEIR LANGUAGE?
EVERY WORD IS A BAD WORD IN SOMEONE'S LANGUAGE, STATISTICALLY SPEAKING.

BUT NO. THIS SEEMS LIKE SOMETHING ELSE.
ALMOST AS IF THEY HAVE SOMETHING TO FEAR...

SORRY. LIKE WE SAID, TOURISTS.
DOES THIS HAPPEN TO BE THE ONE PLACE IN THE WHOLE UNIVERSE WHERE THE CONCEPT OF SANTA IS A NEGATIVE?

ARE YOU CLAIMING TO BE WITH SANTA?

TOURISTS. VERY CURIOUS TOURISTS.
WE JUST HAVE STORIES ABOUT SA--
--THE S MAN. BACK WHERE WE COME FROM.
AND FROM THE DÉCOR WE TOOK YOU AS FANS.

WELL, I BELIEVE IN CHILDREN'S DREAMS. AND LAUGHTER. GENERAL JOLLINESS.
BRINGING JOY TO OTHERS THROUGH SPACE AND TIME, DESPITE IMPOSSIBLE ODDS.
SO IF YOU CONSIDER MY AGREEING WITH THOSE THINGS AS "BEING WITH SANTA", WELL...
...THEN I SUPPOSE I AM.

THAT SOUNDS LIKE A CONFESSION TO ME.

I'M MORE INTERESTED IN HEARING MR. HENDERSON'S THOUGHTS ON THIS.
SINCE HE SEEMS TO BE IN CHARGE HERE.

I HAVE NOTHING TO SAY TO YOU.

AND DON'T THINK I HAVEN'T NOTICED.
FAR SAFER THAT WAY, ISN'T IT?
OTHERWISE YOU RUN THE RISK OF TRIPPING AN OVERWRITTEN MEMORY.

I DON'T HAVE TIME FOR THIS.
LOCK THEM UP AND THEN RETURN TO WORK.

YOU HEARD THE BOSS.
IS THIS HOW YOU TREAT ALL THE WAYWARD TOURISTS?
ARREST AND IMPRISONMENT?
THIS IS A STATE-OF-THE-ART RESEARCH FACILITY.
AND YOU ARE INDUSTRIAL SPIES.
THANK YOU FOR THE INFORMATION.
WHAT KIND OF RESEARCH?
MOVE!

INSIDE!
THINK A LOT OF YOURSELF FOR A BLOKE DRESSED LIKE A TOY, DON'T YOU.
THE ONLY THING THAT MATTERS IS WHAT MR. HENDERSON THINKS OF ME.
CLIK

OH YEAH? ANYONE EVER TELL YOUR BOSS HE LOOKS JUST LIKE SANTA?!

MAY HAVE BEEN A SHADE TOO FAR THERE, RYAN.

SANTA IS THE ONE WHO'S BEEN SNATCHING OUR WORKERS.
QUITE POSSIBLY EATING THEM.

HE'S A MONSTER.

AND SO IS ANYONE WHO WOULD SIDE WITH HIM.

WHAT WAS THAT YOU SAID EARLIER TO MR. HENDERSON?
ABOUT TRIPPING AN OVERWRITTEN MEMORY?
MMM?
IF MR. HENDERSON IS INDEED RESPONSIBLE FOR OUR MEMORY WIPE, THAT MEANS WE WERE HERE BEFORE.
AND THINGS OCCURRING SIMILAR TO *LAST* TIME COULD BREAK THROUGH THE FAKE MEMORIES WE WERE GIVEN.
SNIFF
CAREFUL, DOC! DON'T WANT TO LOSE YOUR NOSE...
MUCH LIKE WITH HUMANS, MY SENSE OF SMELL IS CLOSELY LINKED TO MY MEMORY.
I'VE *DEFINITELY* BEEN HERE BEFORE.
OF COURSE YOU HAVE.

WHO'S THERE?
OH DOCTOR...
...YOU REALLY DON'T REMEMBER, DO YOU?

SO. YOU KNOW WHO I AM.
OF COURSE. I KNOW YOU ALL.
YAZ, RYAN, GRAHAM.
ALL RIGHT, MATE. YOU KNOW OUR NAMES...
...BUT WE DON'T KNOW WHO YOU ARE.
OR WHY WE SHOULD TRUST YOU.
DOESN'T LOOK LIKE YOU HAVE MUCH OF A CHOICE.

AND IF YOU KNOW ME, REALLY KNOW ME, YOU KNOW "DON'T HAVE A CHOICE" WON'T WORK.
WOULD LIKE TO TRUST YOU. HOPE TO TRUST YOU. BUT NOT BECAUSE OF THREATS.
AND THAT SOUNDS LIKE THE DOCTOR I KNOW.
JUST HAD TO BE SURE.
DIDN'T SEE THAT ONE COMING.

STEPPING OUT FROM THE SHADOWS IS A GOOD FIRST STEP.
A NAME WOULD HELP TOO.
THE NAME IS BAXTER.
JEFF SENT ME.
JEFF SENT YOU?!
WHY DIDN'T YOU SAY SO FROM THE START?
I DON'T THINK WE'VE MET A JEFF, HAVE WE?
DOESN'T SOUND FAMILIAR.

HAVE YOU TRIED THE SONIC?
OF COURSE.
DEADLOCK SEAL.
MORE PROOF THAT WE WERE HERE BEFORE, EVEN IF WE DON'T REMEMBER.
VWRRRR
CAN YOU DO SOMETHING TO GET US OUT?
SEEING AS YOU'RE THE ONLY ONE HERE OUTSIDE THE CELL?
I'M A SAFETY OFFICER. SECURITY ISN'T REALLY MY SPECIALTY...
TING TING
SAFETY OFFICER FOR JEFF, THEN?
QUITE.

AH! I THINK I HAVE IT!
PLEASE BACK AWAY FROM THE BARS.
FOR YOUR OWN SAFETY.
OF COURSE, SAFETY OFFICER BAXTER.
HERE GOES NOTHING...
FWOOSH

SMASH

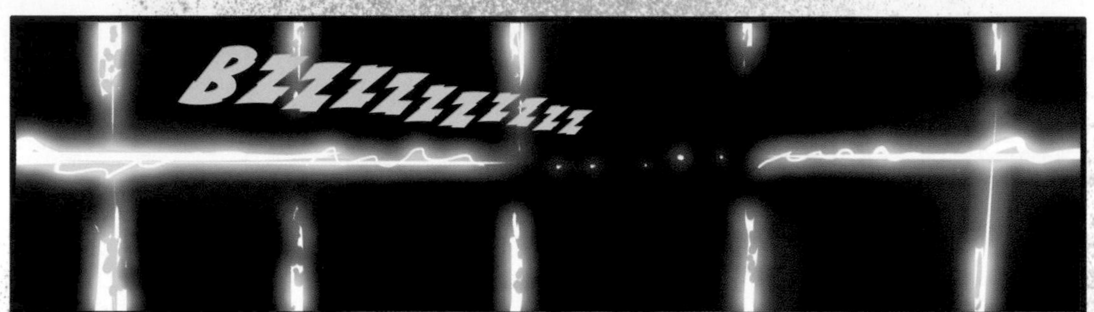
BZZZZZZZZZZ

MUCH BETTER THAN NOTHING, BAXTER.
THANK YOU.

I COULDN'T HELP BUT NOTICE THE POINTED EARS.
ARE YOU, LIKE, A PROPER ELF?

DO YOU HAVE A PROBLEM WITH ELVES?

NO! I JUST MEANT...
...I'VE NEVER MET ONE BEFORE.
EXCEPT IF BAXTER HERE IS RIGHT, THEN YOU HAVE.
CAN YOU EXPLAIN TO US EXACTLY WHAT'S GOING ON HERE?
IT MIGHT BE EASIER IF I SHOW YOU.
FOLLOW ME.

"WELL, IT LOOKS LIKE WE KNOW WHAT HAPPENED TO FRIFFLE'S PEOPLE."
BROUGHT TO THIS WORLD BY MR. HENDERSON TO SERVE AS A LABOR FORCE.
AN ENSLAVED LABOR FORCE, BY THE LOOKS OF THINGS.
THAT'S HOW I'VE BEEN GETTING ABOUT-- DISGUISED AS A WORKER.
WE ALL LOOK THE SAME TO HIM...

DOCTOR, LOOK!
DOES THAT MEAN OUR MEMORIES ARE BEING ERASED AGAIN?
I DO HAVE A BIT OF A HEADACHE.
IF IT WAS STRONG ENOUGH TO BE AFFECTING OUR MINDS, THE GLOW WOULD BE FAR BRIGHTER.
BUT IT IS NEARBY...
VWRRRRR

OH NO...
IT'S DOWN THERE. THEY'RE USING IT ON THE WORKERS.
VERY DARK CRYSTAL OF 'EM.
DO YOU THINK WE TRIED TO SHUT IT OFF LAST TIME WE WERE HERE?
AND IT BACKFIRED ON US?
THAT WOULD EXPLAIN MISSING MEMORIES, YES.
BUT OURS WERE OVERWRITTEN. AND THAT IMPLIES INTENT. SOMEONE WITH SOMETHING TO HIDE.

HEY, WHAT ARE THOSE TWO SAYING?
...WANTS THE COLD FUSION REACTOR READY BY CHRISTMAS.
THE ELVES WILL HAVE TO WORK A FEW EXTRA SHIFTS IF WE'RE GOING TO...
THEY'RE TALKING ABOUT MAKING COLD FUSION?
THAT WOULD BE A GOOD THING, YEAH?
IT WOULD BE, YES. BUT THAT'S NOT COLD FUSION TECH THEY'RE BUILDING DOWN THERE.
I'M NOT SURE ***WHAT*** IT IS.
YOU BEEN UNDERCOVER FOR A WHILE NOW, RIGHT? DON'T ***YOU*** KNOW?
AFTER YOUR LAST VISIT WENT AWRY, I'VE HAD TO KEEP A LOW PROFILE.

DO YOU KNOW THE WAY TO MR. HENDERSON'S OFFICE?
ONE SECOND...

AH! YES. NOT TOO FAR.
FOLLOW ME, PLEASE.

MIND THE NEUROLOGICAL TRACKERS. THEY'LL LET US KNOW IF THERE ARE ANY MIND TRAPS ALONG THE WAY.

GOT IT.

I DO HAVE ONE QUESTION, DOC.
AND MAYBE IT ISN'T MY PLACE TO ASK...

WHAT IS IT, GRAHAM?

BAXTER'S BOSS, YOUR FRIEND, JEFF...
IS HE, BY CHANCE... SANTA?

WHAT KIND OF NAME IS JEFF FOR SOMEONE LIKE SANTA?

I SUPPOSE IT IS A BIT... ORDINARY.

THIS WAY, EVERYONE.

I BET THE CORSAIR WOULD LOVE THIS.
IF THERE *WAS* A SANTA, I BET THE CORSAIR WOULD HAVE ALREADY ROBBED HIM.
SEVERAL TIMES OVER.
IF THERE WERE A SANTA CLAUS, I'M SURE HE'D HAVE *EXCEPTIONAL* SECURITY.

EXCELLENT CRAFTSMANSHIP.
WHAT EXACTLY ARE WE LOOKING FOR IN HERE?
CLUES, EVIL PLANS, HIDDEN CANDY STASH.
THE USUAL.
UH. DOCTOR?

DID YOU FIND THE CANDY?
OH. HMM.
IT MAY NOT BE TIME LORD TECHNOLOGY...
...BUT IT IS BIGGER ON THE INSIDE.

LISTEN TO THIS.

"DYLAN FRY, AGE SEVEN."
"JORDAN FRY, AGE FOUR."
"LILY JENKINS, AGE TEN."
KIDS NAMES AND AGES. HUNDREDS AND HUNDREDS OF THEM.
IS THIS LIST NAUGHTY OR NICE?
NEVER BEEN ON THE NAUGHTY LIST, ME.
IS THAT A FACT?

SO WE HAVE A BUNCH OF SANTA SUITS AND A LIST OF CHILDREN.
ARE WE *SURE* THIS ISN'T SANTA WE'RE DEALING WITH?

VERY SURE.

SOMEONE TAKING ADVANTAGE OF THE MYTH, THOUGH.
IF IT *IS* A MYTH.

ONE THING'S FOR SURE. WE NEED TO--
KLIK
HIDE. WE NEED TO HIDE.

COME ON, IN HERE.

DMF
CREEK
NOW WHERE DID I LEAVE...
AH. EXCELLENT.
EVERYTHING IS GOING ACCORDING TO PLAN.
BUT THAT'S--

AND SOON IT WILL BE TIME FOR THE CHRISTMAS FEAST!

ZEEP

MISTRESS?

IT IS NEARLY TIME. ARE THEY GATHERED?
YES, MISTRESS.

THE COSTUMES ARE IN THERE. GATHER THEM.
I WILL MAKE THE FINAL PREPARATIONS FOR THE MACHINE.

THWAK!
WHAT ON EARTH IS THAT?
NOT ON EARTH, FOR ONE.
IT'S A MINION OF KRAMPUS.
OUR DEAR MR. HENDERSON ISN'T AT ALL WHO THEY SEEM.

KRAMPUS? YOU MEAN THE SORT OF ANTI-SANTA?
IT'S REAL?

I HAD MY SUSPICIONS. EVEN BEFORE YOUR FIRST VISIT.
BUT NOW I HAVE PROOF.

I WOULD SUSPECT YOU'RE THE EXPERT ON KRAMPUS HERE, BAXTER.
WHAT CAN YOU TELL US?
THE STORIES SAY THAT KRAMPUS VISITS BAD CHILDREN ON CHRISTMAS. BUT REALLY, ANY CHILD WILL DO.
SHE FEEDS ON FEAR. AND WHOSE FEAR IS MORE PURE AND UNRESTRAINED BY LOGIC THAN A CHILD'S?
IRONICALLY, SHE CONSIDERS HERSELF A VEGETARIAN. SINCE SHE ONLY CONSUMES ENERGY AND NOT FLESH.
SO SHE DOESN'T *EAT* THE CHILDREN. I SUPPOSE THAT'S A PLUS?
SO HOW DO WE STOP HER?
FOLLOW ME, FAM.
LET'S SAVE CHRISTMAS.

SOON, MY CHILDREN. HUNDREDS OF DEMONIC SANTAS, TERRIFYING THE LOVE OF CHRISTMAS OUT OF THE CHILDREN OF EARTH.
A FEAST FOR THE AGES. AND A FEAR THAT WILL LAST A LIFETIME.
WELL THAT SOUNDS AWFUL.
REGULAR GRINCH, SHE IS.
AND THESE ARE GLOWING AGAIN.
OF COURSE.
KRAMPUS HAS THE WORKERS IN THERE BELIEVING THEY'RE BUILDING A COLD FUSION DEVICE.
LOOKS LIKE IT'S A HYBRID TELEPORTATION AND ENERGY COLLECTION DEVICE. THAT'S WHY THE COMPONENTS LOOKED SO STRANGE.
IT WASN'T JUST ONE THING THEY WERE BUILDING HERE.
AND IT LOOKS LIKE WE ONLY HAVE A FEW MINUTES UNTIL IT'S DECEMBER 25TH ON THE INTERNATIONAL DATE LINE.
WE HAVE TO HURRY.

HOLD ON, YAZ. IF YOU GO STRAIGHT IN THERE, YOU'LL BE SUBJECT TO THE MIND REWRITE ALL OVER AGAIN.
YOU'LL NEED TO SHUT THE MACHINE DOWN FROM OUT HERE...
HERE. IT WILL SERVE AS A GOOD DISTRACTION WHILE I REROUTE THE TELEPORT.
BUT THEN WON'T *YOUR* MEMORY BE REWRITTEN?
BROUGHT THIS IN CASE OF AN EMERGENCY.
SHOULD BLOCK THE EFFECTS OF KRAMPUS'S DEVICE FOR A COUPLE MINUTES, AT LEAST.
ACTIVATE THE SONIC WHEN I GIVE YOU THE SIGNAL. IT SHOULD SHORT OUT THE MIND CONTROL.
BAXTER, YOU'LL KEEP THEM SAFE?
OF COURSE, DOCTOR.

VWRRRRR

ZUMMMMMMMM
WHAT?!
WHAT AM I WEARING?!
WHERE AM I?
WHAT'S GOING ON?
IS IT CHRISTMAS?
YOU GETTING THAT TOO?
MY MEMORIES...
OW.
AND THIS CONNECTS TO THIS...
RRRARGGH
SO MUCH EASIER WITH THE SONIC...

YOU PERSIST IN VEXING ME?!
YEAH.
KIND OF OUR THING.

IT IS MY DUTY AS SAFETY OFFICER TO ENSURE THAT ALL INNOCENTS ARE SAFE FROM YOUR PLOTTING, KRAMPUS.

YOU REALLY THINK THAT YOU CAN STOP WHAT I'VE SET IN MOTION?
MY ARMY WILL SET FORTH AND--
EXCUSE ME...

WHAT ARMY WAS THAT?

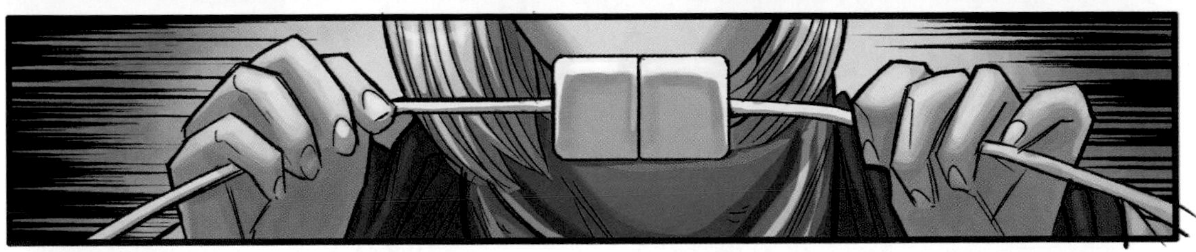

NO!

THIS ISN'T OVER, DOCTOR!

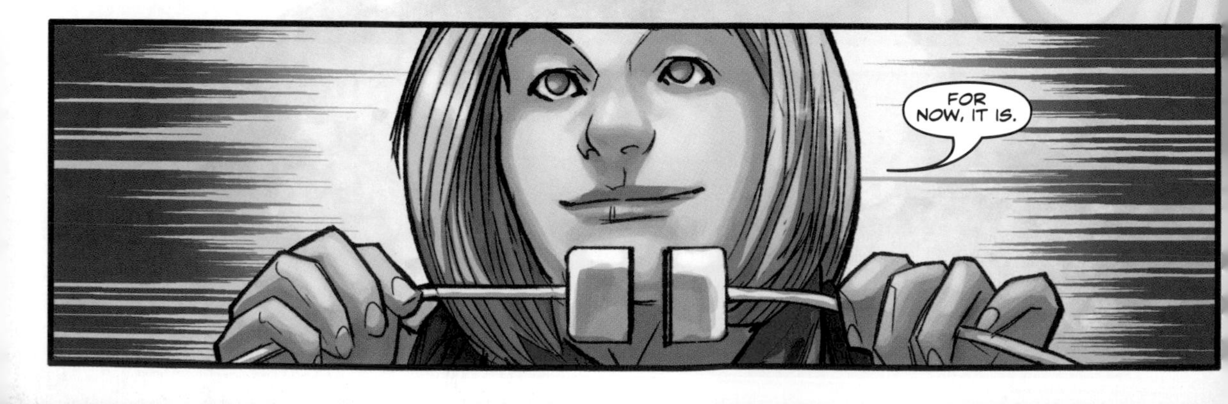
FOR NOW, IT IS.

WERE... WERE THOSE...
ARE THOSE--

ALIENS! CONGRATULATIONS, YOU DISCOVERED THEM!
EXCEPT NOT REALLY. THEY'VE BEEN AROUND FOR AGES.

WHO ARE YOU?
DO YOU KNOW WHAT'S GOING ON?
ARE ALIENS TAKING OVER?
WHAT DO YOU MEAN AGES?
I CAN TELL YOU HAVE A LOT OF QUESTIONS. HAPPY TO DEAL WITH THAT.
BUT FIRST THINGS FIRST.
WHO HERE IS A GOOD COOK?
I'LL ACCEPT MIDDLING IF WE'RE DESPERATE.

PERFECT!
I ASSUME THIS PLACE HAS KITCHENS, IF SOMEONE COULD SHOW ME THE WAY?
ARE WE COOKING SOMETHING, DOC?
OF COURSE.
CHRISTMAS DINNER!

HELLO, I'M THE DOCTOR. THERE ARE A LOT OF YOU IN THIS ROOM I HAVEN'T MET BEFORE TODAY.
AND I MAY NOT BE EXACTLY THE PERSON YOU EXPECTED TO SPEND CHRISTMAS WITH.
BUT THAT'S THE BEAUTY OF THE HOLIDAYS, ISN'T IT? SOMETIMES, THINGS GO WRONG IN THE BEST WAY.
AND YOU FIND YOURSELF AT DINNER WITH EVERYONE -- FROM YOUR VERY BEST FRIENDS TO THE MONSTER IN THE CABINET.
BUT IN THE END, DOES IT REALLY MATTER WHERE ANY OF US CAME FROM?
JUST BEING HERE, CARING AND COOKING AND HELPING, SITTING DOWN TOGETHER TO SHARE IN THIS...
...THAT'S WHAT IT'S ALWAYS BEEN ABOUT.
TO UNEXPECTED FRIENDS!

IF I COULD ASK JUST ONE QUESTION...
ALWAYS.

WELL, IF KRAMPUS, THE ANTI-SANTA, IS ACTUALLY REAL...
...DOES THAT MEAN SANTA IS TOO?

NOW, THAT WOULD BE TELLING...

EPILOGUE
POLICE PUBLIC CALL BOX
THERE. JUST RIGHT.
POLICE TELEPHONE
FREE FOR USE OF PUBLIC
ADVICE & ASSISTANCE OBTAINABLE IMMEDIATELY
OFFICERS & CARS RESPOND TO URGENT CALLS
PULL TO OPEN
AND CAN'T FORGET...
HAPPY CHRISTMAS, OLD FRIEND.
THE END...?

BBC

DOCTOR WHO

THE THIRTEENTH DOCTOR

Covers Gallery

FREE COMIC BOOK DAY 2019 • WILL BROOKS

ISSUE #1 COVER A • CLAUDIA CARANFA

ISSUE #2 COVER A • CLAUDIA CARANFA

ISSUE #1 COVER B • WILL BROOKS

ISSUE #2 COVER B • WILL BROOKS

BBC

DOCTOR WHO

From a friend! -?

WITH SONIC SCREWDRIVER

THIRTEENTH DOCTOR

ACTION FIGURE

ISSUE #1 COVER C • BLAIR SHEDD

BBC

DOCTOR WHO

POLICE PUBLIC CALL BOX

POLICE TELEPHONE
FREE FOR
USE OF PUBLIC
ADVICE & ASSISTANCE OBTAINABLE IMMEDIATELY
OFFICERS & CARS RESPOND TO URGENT CALLS
PULL TO OPEN

From a friend! -?

INCLUDES
LIGHT-UP
LANTERN!

THE TARDIS
ELECTRONIC TARDIS PLAYSET

ISSUE #2 COVER C • BLAIR SHEDD

BBC
DOCTOR WHO

READER'S GUIDE

With so many amazing *Doctor Who* collections already on the shelves, it
be difficult to know where to start. That's where this handy guide comes
And don't be overwhelmed – every collection is designed to be welcomi
whatever your knowledge of *Doctor Who*.

THE TWELFTH DOCTOR

VOL. 1: TERRORFORMER

VOL. 2: FRACTURES

VOL. 3: HYPERION

YEAR TWO BEGINS! VOL. 4: SCHOOL OF DEATH

VOL. 5: THE TWIST

THE ELEVENTH DOCTOR

VOL. 1: AFTER LIFE

VOL. 2: SERVE YOU

VOL. 3: CONVERSION

YEAR TWO BEGINS! VOL. 4: THE THEN AND THE NOW

VOL. 5: THE ONE

THE TENTH DOCTOR

VOL. 1: REVOLUTIONS OF TERROR

VOL. 2: THE WEEPING ANGELS OF MONS

VOL. 3: THE FOUNTAINS OF FOREVER

YEAR TWO BEGINS! VOL. 4: THE ENDLESS SONG

VOL. 5: ARENA OF FEAR

THE NINTH DOCTOR

VOL. 1: WEAPONS OF PAST DESTRUCTION

VOL. 2: DOCTORMANIA

VOL. 3: OFFICIAL SECRETS

VOL. 4: SIN EATERS

Each comic series is entirely self-contained and focused on one Doctor, so you can follow one, two, or all of your favorite Doctors, as you wish! The series are arranged in TV season-like Years, collected into roughly three collections per Year. Feel free to start at Volume 1 of any series, or jump straight to the volumes labelled in blue! Each book, and every comic, features a catch-up and character guide at the beginning, making it easy to jump on board – and each comic series has a very different flavor, representative of that Doctor's era on screen. If in doubt, set the TARDIS Randomizer and dive in wherever you land!

VOL. 6:
SONIC BOOM

YEAR THREE BEGINS!
TIME TRIALS VOL. 1:
THE TERROR BENEATH

TIME TRIALS VOL. 2:
THE WOLVES
OF WINTER

TIME TRIALS VOL. 3:
A CONFUSION OF
ANGELS

THE THIRTEENTH DOCTOR

THE MANY
LIVES OF

THE ROAD TO THE
THIRTEENTH DOCTOR

VOL. 6:
THE MALIGNANT TRUTH

YEAR THREE BEGINS!
THE SAPLING VOL. 1:
GROWTH

THE SAPLING VOL. 2:
ROOTS

THE SAPLING VOL. 3:
BRANCHES

VOL. 1:
A NEW
BEGINNING

VOL. 2:
HIDDEN HUMAN
HISTORY

VOL. 3:
OLD FRIENDS

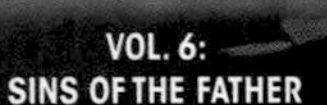

VOL. 6:
SINS OF THE FATHER

VOL. 7:
WAR OF GODS

YEAR THREE BEGINS!
FACING FATE VOL. 1:
BREAKFAST AT TYRANNY'S

FACING FATE VOL. 2:
VORTEX BUTTERFLIES

FACING FATE VOL. 3:
THE GOOD COMPANION

CLASSIC DOCTORS

THIRD DOCTOR:
THE HERALDS OF
DESTRUCTION

FOURTH DOCTOR:
GAZE OF THE
MEDUSA

SEVENTH DOCTOR:
OPERATION
VOLCANO

EIGHTH DOCTOR:
A MATTER OF LIFE
AND DEATH

MULTI-DOCTOR EVENTS

FOUR
DOCTORS

SUPREMACY OF
THE CYBERMEN

THE LOST
DIMENSION
(BOOKS ONE & TWO)

BBC

DOCTOR WHO

THE THIRTEENTH DOCTOR

Biographies

Jody Houser

is a prolific writer of comics, perhaps best known for her work on *Faith* and *Mother Panic*. She has also written *Star Wars: Rogue One, Star Wars: Age of Republic, Amazing Spider-Man: Renew Your Vows, Spider-Girls, The X-Files: Origins, Orphan Black, Stranger Things, StarCraft*, and *Halo*.

Roberta Ingranata

is an Italian comic artist. She worked for various Italian publishers before making the leap to US comics. Titles she has leant her considerable talents to include the highly acclaimed *Witchblade* series, *Robyn Hood*, and *Van Helsing*.

Enrica Eren Angiolini

is a colorist and illustrator from Italy. Enrica's rich colors go from strength to strength, as demonstrated by her work on *Warhammer 40,000, Shades of Magic: The Steel Prince*, and her cover work for Titan Comics, Dark Horse, and Aspen Comics.

Tracy Bailey

is a colorist who has worked on many exciting projects for Titan Comics, including *Fighting American* and *Tank Girl Colour Classics*, in which she colored artist Jamie Hewlett's original B&W art for the very first time.